Norma "d Bandit"
2008

BANDIT

"A Raccoon Tail"

My true story told in first person

Norma Louise Lapierre

BANDIT

"A Raccoon Tail"

My true story told in first person

Written by:
Norma Louise Lapierre

Design and layout by:
Andrew Adams

Acknowledgements

A very special thank you to my husband for his help and the many hours he spent listening and helping me edit. His suggestions were invaluable.

For Bandit, may she live a long and happy life and add many more raccoons for the world to enjoy!
&
For all our family and friends who have lovingly enjoyed Bandit's life with us and first-handedly seen her and laughed at her antics.

Thank you to Andrew Adams, a high school student who knows far more than I about computers. He spent many countless hours on his personal computer putting the photographs and copy together.

A special thank you to a local, licensed rehabber for allowing us to become her foster parents.

Copyright © 2008 by Norma Louise Lapierre. 44457-LAPI
Library of Congress Control Number: 2007908489
ISBN: Softcover 978-1-4257-9476-7
Hardcover 978-1-4257-9492-7

Norma L. Lapierre
www.mgtdginger@aol.com

This book was printed in the United States of America.

Dedication

*T*his photographic narrative is dedicated
to everyone, young and old, who has a "soft spot"
in their hearts for any of
God's creatures.

We are all
linked together in some way!

Here I am as a wee baby Kit born
in the rainy month of April.
I'm all curled up in a tiny ball,
sound asleep,
weighing in at a few ounces and 7" long
including my ringed tail.
My eyes are tightly closed,
not to open for a month.

I spent much of my early childhood
sleeping on towels and pillows.
See how long my legs are?
Notice my tongue is just barely visible as I lay sleeping
I have no noticeable hump on my back - yet!

My Kennel Cab was my home for 3 months. Mom and Dad put a log in the back to separate my living quarters from the towel-lined front. I had two small bowls - one for water, one for food. The bedding was changed daily.

I'm very cautiously climbing out of my home onto the floor. Remember, I cannot see or hear!

In order to get around, I carefully follow the scent of Mom and Dad's feet.

Mom is lying on the
floor playing with me.
You can see how tiny I really am.
She smells so good. I have "imprinted" on
both my human Mother and Father.

Both my adoptive human parents take turns feeding me my formula 5 - 6 times a day.

However, I did sleep through the night!

Dad is my second caregiver.
His chest is so warm and his hair
reminds me of my raccoon Mom. See,
have five fingers with opposing thumbs and toes, just like you.

Mom is feeding me my bottle.
I'm so cute, but maybe
a bib would help!

Now that my eyes are open,
you can see my teeth coming in.
I love chewing on the rubber
nipple of my bottle.

I was able ___ ___
outside afte ___
could see ___el___
Mom's ___
H___s___s___
The le___ves
and fl___e's
were all f___
game ___ ___

See me hiding behind
the blue wooden
angel leg in Mom's garden.

Now that my eyes are open, the kitchen and family room became my new playground.

Dad's banjo made a great "plinking" sound.

The water in the dishwasher was just too tempting.

It took me two months to crawl up on this bowl of pens and pencils.

The chimenera on
their patio
was a great
place to play.
I loved the smell
of the
burnt wood.
Of course I was
covered with
ashes.

This is the house my Dad built for me. He wouldn't let me help paint, but I did "supervise".

I ate and slept there when I was little, when my parents were outside to protect me.

This is a great personal picture of my human siste[r]
Lisa and her daughter, Shannon.
Of my nine human nieces and nephews,
she was the first to see me.

This plant was usually covered with flowers... not after I was done playing with them.

The accumulated water in the cup holder in the arm of the chair was just my size— as was the chair.

One of my favorite positions is
lying on my back.
Not the most graceful,
but I can see everything
that is going on!

I'm playing
"Peek-a-Boo"
behind a
pillow on
the couch.

One warm, sunny afternoon during a patio outing,
crawled up on Dad's shoulder and fell fast asleep for
almost two hours! I was so comfortable.
Dad did complain about cramps in his back;
however, he never moved.

This is an
empty flower pot.
I thought it
was just my size.

Here is a patio excursion. Mom is spraying me with the hos
How I love water!

One day I climbed into the washing machine. There was only a tiny bit of water in it. Mom snapped a picture of me. It looks like I have a Yarmulke on my head!

The shelf with cookbooks on it smelled so sweet. I couldn't resist climbing up there and knocking them all on the floor. I really wasn't going to eat them. I think Mom got tired of cleaning up after me!!

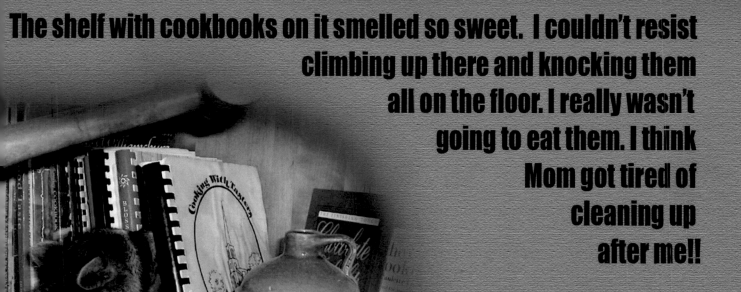

I say "Grace" before eating.
See my folded paws.

I'm getting bigger now.
I love all the crinkling
noises of Mom's
umbrella stand.

Dad is feeding
me a pretzel-
a favorite treat.

The tub! Water! This is my own private basket full of toys.
Notice the dripping faucet. I even take weekly showers
with Mom in the tub.
 The little rivulets
of water running
down the
shower
curtain were
just too
much to
endure.
So in
I went!

Eating is my favorite pastime.

The water helps soften my food.

Sometimes I'm hand fed.

I especially love all kinds of nuts!

I eat dog food, potato chips, and sandwich cookies.

I'm not very neat.

Now I'm getting
bigger and am
allowed to go
outside more often.

Trees of any size
are fair game.
I especially
like the
wood pile!

Night time is my time to play, remember I'm nocturnal.

Playing "Hide and Seek" or "Biting Their Hands Through the Sheets" are my two favorite games.

I'm very gentle and don't hurt them.

Mom and Dad's closet is a fun place to play.

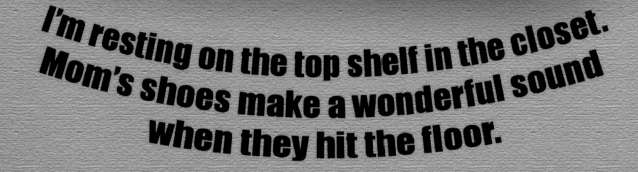

I'm resting on the top shelf in the closet.
Mom's shoes make a wonderful sound
when they hit the floor.

This Austin Healy became my second home during the winter. It's up on a car lift.
A ladder was provided so
I could go up and down.

I must keep up with
the "news", so here I am resting on
the back of the couch,
apparently reading
the newspaper.

Christmas Time!

No, I never climbed their tree, but I did play with the Christmas tree balls. They hung from the lower branches. Only six were broken!

Here I am playing with Mom's hair. Why is she hiding her face?

Dad's pockets are full of treasures- coins, keys and sometimes nuts!

I'm fully grown now and almost two years old. "There's no place like home" certainly is true and I return nightly for the best chow and to play with my parents. I've even had all my shots and a flea bath, just like a dog or cat. I have the best of both the animal AND human worlds.

Epilogue

Our true story has not yet ended. We continue to live with and thoroughly enjoy our "fifth" child. She is like one of our own. As our four children have grown, married and have their own children, Bandit has filled a void in our lives. We always felt that God has an "Orphaned Animal Book" in Heaven. As He is thumbing through the pages looking for adoptive human parents, He comes across our name. He sees that we currently have no pets, of which we have had many, and as Bandit was only 5 days old, selected us as the perfect humans to care for one of His needy creatures.

Bandit has had all the same shots necessary for a domesticated animal. Plus she's had medication for fleas, ticks, worms and even a large injury on her nose, so she is very safe for us to handle. Our wild animal rehabber warned us not to introduce her to another area, as raccoons are very territorial and would not be receptive to an interloper. We took his advice.

She has returned to the wild and comes to see us most nights for food, affection, play and even sometimes a few hours of sleep. We are her only known "Mom and Dad" and we graciously accept this challenge.

The joy this single animal has brought to us is unsurpassed!